WORLD OF

MAMMALS

WHALES

By Sophie Lockwood

Content Adviser: Barbara E. Brown, Scientific Associate, Mammal Division, Field Museum of Chicago

THE CHILD'S WORLD®, MANKATO, MINNESOTA

Whales

Published in the United States of America by The Child's World®
1980 Lookout Drive • Mankato, MN 56003-1705
800-599-READ • www.childsworld.com

Acknowledgements:

The Child's World®: Mary Berendes, Publishing Director

The Creative Spark: Mary Francis, Project Director; Wendy Mead, Editor; Deborah Goodsite, Photo Researcher

The Design Lab: Kathleen Petelinsek, Designer and Production Artist

Photos:

Cover: Daniel J Cox/Photographer's Choice/Getty Images; frontispiece and page 4: Jon Helgason/iStockphoto.com; half title: Jim Parkin/iStockphoto.com.

Interior: Alamy: 5 top right and 15 (Douglas Fisher), 5 bottom right and 37 (Woodfall Wild Images); Animals Animals: 5 top left and 10 (Bob Cranston); The Bridgeman Art Library: 33 (Gavin Graham Gallery, London, UK), 34 (Whaling (engraving on ivory of sperm whale), American School, (20th century)/Private Collection, Archives Charmet); Jupiterimages: 19 (Doug Allan/Oxford Scientific); Minden Pictures: 9 (Frans Lanting), 13, 16–17 photo obtained under N.M.F.S. Permit #987, 22 (Flip Nicklin), 5 bottom right and 28, 31 (Todd Pusser/npl); Photolibrary Group: 25, 26; Photo Researchers, Inc.: 5 center left and 21 (Francois Gohier).

Library of Congress Cataloging-in-Publication Data

Lockwood, Sophie.
  Whales / by Sophie Lockwood.
    p. cm. — (The world of mammals)
  Includes index.
  ISBN 978-1-59296-930-2 (library bound : alk. paper)
  1. Whales—Juvenile literature. I. Title. II. Series.
  QL737.C4L64 2008
  599.5—dc22   2007020890

TABLE OF CONTENTS

Chapter One

A Magnificent Journey

A female gray whale dives in the Bering Sea, Alaska. Rolling onto her right side, she scoops up **sediment** and water from the seafloor. By sifting the mixture through her **baleen,** she collects her daily meal of marine worms, **amphipods,** and small **crustaceans.** The water, sand, and mud that is left over pours out the side of her mouth. For the past four months, she has devoured about 1,090 kilograms (2,400 pounds) of food daily. As she feeds, a cloud of gray-brown **silt** pours from her mouth. The trail can be seen for miles.

Tomorrow, she begins a magnificent journey southward to a bay in Baja California. Our cow is pregnant, and she will travel in a pod of five other mothers-to-be. Their journey will take them 10,000 kilometers (6,200 miles) southward. At a cruising speed of 3.2 to 9.6 kilometers per

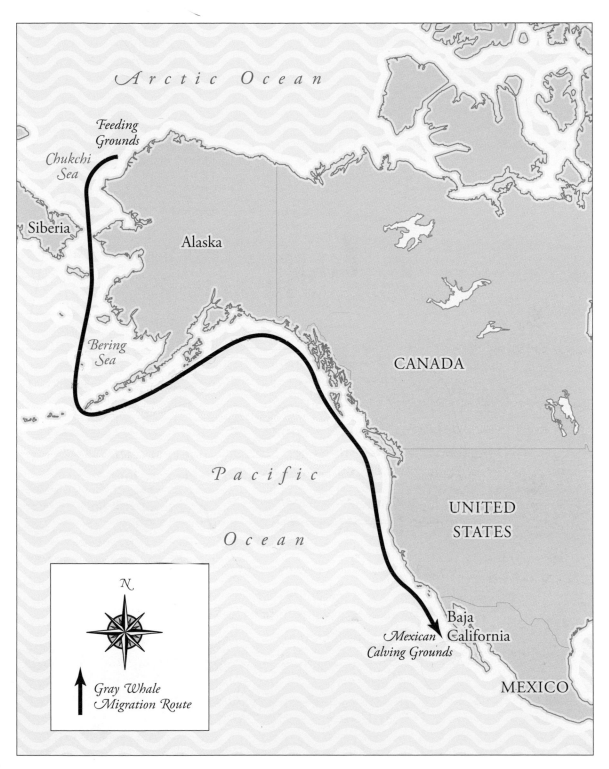

This is the migration route of the gray whales that live off the coast of North America.

hour (2 to 6 miles per hour), it should take about three months to reach Scammon's Lagoon, a favorite destination for gray whales to spend the winter.

Our gray whale cow became sexually mature when she reached 11 or 12 meters (36 to 39.4 feet) long. She was about seven years old at the time. She now weighs 30 metric tons (33 tons).

Our mother is reaching the end of her eleventh month of pregnancy. After she reaches Scammon's Lagoon, she delivers a female calf. The calf is no tiny baby. It measures 4.5 meters (14.8 feet) long and weighs 500 kilograms (1,100 pounds). Mother and child stay in Mexican waters for at least two months. During that time, baby will put on a thick layer of blubber. She needs the fat to stay warm when the whales return to Alaskan waters. While in Mexico, the mother does not eat. The food supply is not sufficient in the lagoon. The mother simply goes hungry until she reaches the Bering Sea, five months after her child is born.

Today, the world's gray whale population is estimated at 26,000. Estimating a whale species' population is neither easy nor accurate. Whales do not gather in motionless groups to be counted. These 26,000 gray whales live in two

populations: an endangered population in Japanese waters and a recovered population along North America's West Coast. Once, both populations were endangered. However, legal protection of the North American whales has allowed that population to rebound. A third population once lived in the North Atlantic but has been **extinct** since the eighteenth century.

The only possible protection for gray whales is a ban on whaling. While smaller mammals can be captured and bred in zoos

A young gray whale and its mother swim in the waters off the coast of Mexico.

Would You Believe?
Whale milk is 53 percent fat and is filled with calcium and phosphorous. These three ingredients help a nursing calf gain weight fast. Drinking about 190 liters (50 gallons) of milk a day, a nursing calf puts on a few pounds every hour it nurses.

and aquariums, gray whales are much too large. In 1971, a gray whale that keepers named Gigi was found as a deserted infant. Gigi measured a small 5.5 meters (18 feet) long at the time. Within a year, Gigi was 8.23 meters (27 feet) long and weighed 6.35 metric tons (7 tons). She had outgrown her space. Keepers released Gigi into the sea in March 1972, and she joined a pod of **migrating** gray whales. Seven years later, Gigi was spotted again, this time heading north with her own calf by her side.

Did You Know?
A male whale is called a bull. A female is a cow, and her young are calves. Groups of whales are called pods.

A gray whale passes through kelp in the Pacific Ocean off California on its way south.

Chapter Two

Thar She Blows!

Most books and movies that deal with whales feature the phrase, "Thar she blows!" The phrase refers to a whale's spout when it is taking a breath. Whalers looked for the spout to locate whales on the open seas. Blue whales, the largest whale species, create spouts up to 12 meters (39.4 feet) high.

Unlike fish, whales have lungs and breathe air—just like other mammals. Baleen whales have two blowholes or nostrils. Toothed whales have only one. Blowholes are found on top of whale heads. When rising to take a breath, the area with the blowhole breaks the water first. When the whale dives, the blowhole closes so water does not leak in.

Whales expel waste gas and replace it with oxygen in their lungs. This process exchanges 80 percent of the whale's lung capacity with one breath. The whales blow out carbon dioxide and water vapor and inhale oxygen. They also store oxygen well in their bodies. Size for size, whales have more blood in their bodies than other mammals. This extra blood stores

Did You Know?
Blue whales can grow up to 33.5 meters (110 feet) long and weigh as much as 181 metric tons (399,037 pounds).

oxygen and allows whales to hold their breath longer and dive deeper than other marine mammals.

A whale is shaped much like a torpedo. Its body shape allows it to move easily through the water. Body shape, flippers, and **flukes** make whales agile swimmers. Flippers help with steering, much like paddles help steer a canoe. The flukes, or lobes on whale tails, lie perpendicular to the spine, while fish tails lie in line with the spine. Flukes propel the whales.

CLASSIFYING WHALES

Whales are classified as either baleen whales or toothed whales. Baleen whales have a screen or filter made of fiber similar to human fingernails. Rows of baleen sift food from seawater. Typical food on the baleen whale's menu include **krill,** sardines, amphipods, and other creatures that fall under the term **zooplankton.** Baleen whales swim through the zooplankton with their mouths open. Their tongues force the water out of their mouths, while the baleen filters out the food. Zooplankton swim in clusters or swarms, which makes it easy for a whale to scoop up large quantities.

Baleen whales reach their massive size by eating animals smaller than a baby's pinky finger. A blue whale eats up

to 3,500 kilograms (7,715 pounds) of krill a day. At just over 1 gram (0.035 ounces) each, that's about 3.5 million krill.

Baleen, shown here on a humpback whale, acts as a food filter.

Toothed whales feed on larger sea creatures. Sperm whales, the largest of the toothed whales, have an equally large favorite food—giant squid. To get this food, they dive deep into the ocean. Older sperm whales often have scars around their mouths and heads. The scars are shaped like the suckers on squid tentacles. They are battle scars from fights between the whales and squid.

Many toothed whales hunt using **echolocation,** which is the same technique used by bats to find prey in the dark. The whales emit a sound and interpret the echo that returns. They can determine the size, shape, and distance to the item by the echo bounced off it. They can tell if the item is moving or not. A moving item is most likely prey. Sperm whales find giant squid using echolocation.

Other toothed whales, such as belugas and narwhals, also eat squid, but they eat the smaller variety that rises to the ocean's surface at night. They also eat schooling fish, such as cod and halibut.

Most toothed whales have a full mouth of teeth, although some have teeth just on the bottom. Whale teeth are shaped like cones. Strap-toothed whales have only two lower teeth, which wrap around their jaws. The teeth prevent the whale from opening its mouth fully. The tusk on

a narwhal is also a tooth. It is a male's left tooth, and it grows to 2 to 3 meters (6.7 to 9.8 feet) long.

This photograph shows a sperm whale's teeth and lower jaw.

Did You Know?
Only whales and elephants have brains larger than humans'. Whale brains reached this huge size about 30 million years ago.

A humpback whale approaches a hydrophone, one of the devices that scientists use to listen to whale sounds.

MAKING SENSE OF SOUNDS

Both toothed and baleen whales have an excellent sense of hearing. They can hear sounds from many miles away. A fin whale sends out low-frequency pulses off the coast of North Carolina. That whale's message is heard as far as 850 kilometers (528 miles) away by fin whales swimming off the coasts of Nova Scotia, Bermuda, and Puerto Rico.

Toothed whales have open ear canals, but they may hear sound through their skull bones. Baleen whales have waxlike plugs in their ear canals. Scientists believe that sound is carried through the wax plug.

Whales are highly intelligent. They communicate through grunts, groans, squeaks, squeals, and rumbles. Several species sing to attract mates. Many species also warn each other of danger. Scientists have studied whale communication with little success. We may never know what whales are saying, but we know they are saying something.

Would You Believe?
Whales belong to the Cetacea order, or group, along with dolphins and porpoises. Cetaceans are the fastest swimmers in the seas, clocking up to 33 kilometers per hour (21 miles per hour). Whales propel themselves by moving their flukes up and down.

17

Chapter Three

A Long, Full Life

For whales, the mother provides food, companionship, and protection. She is parent, friend, and teacher. Female whales can be pregnant for nine to seventeen months, depending on the species of whale. The most dangerous time for a calf is during its birth. It might be killed by predators. Then calves must surface immediately to breathe air or they will drown. Once born, growth is rapid. A blue whale calf, during seven months of nursing, will put on 15.4 metric tons (17 tons).

Although young calves bond with their mothers, whales do not form tight-knit families. A calf may never meet its father. Before they turn one year old, baleen whales have been weaned. After that, they may have little contact with their mothers. One exception to this is the strong bond found between right whale mothers and their children.

Toothed whales stay with their mothers until they reach sexual maturity. Toothed-whale mothers may nurse their calves for two years or even longer. Elderly sperm cows have been known to still nurse the last calves they birthed for up to fifteen years.

PODS

The social unit for many whale species is the pod. Belugas may form pods with as many as two hundred whales living and feeding together, although twenty-five is more common. Humpback and fin whales might have ten whales in a pod, while sei and minke whales may just collect in groups of three or so.

A large pod of beluga whales gathers near Somerset Island in Canada.

Did You Know?
Belugas are extremely chatty. They tweet, click, squeak, and squeal, which is why they are sometimes called "sea canaries."

Pod size changes according to the habits of each whale species. Belugas and narwhals live in the same areas and eat similar foods. They often can be seen traveling in mixed-species pods. Humpback whales form loose groups with whales changing from one pod to another regularly. Blue whales like to be alone. A blue whale pod would have only two whales.

BEHAVIORS

Whales have a number of behaviors that are natural in the wild but also entertain visitors at aquariums. The big splash in the aquarium tank comes when a whale breaches. Breaching is jumping high out of the water, then slapping down hard. Some whales twist about when breaching. Others simply leap and splash repeatedly. The purpose behind breaching is unknown. It may be to loosen skin parasites or just to play. Spyhopping occurs when a whale pokes its head out of the water and takes a look around. Lobtailing involves slapping the water's surface with the flukes. It's loud and wet and probably announces danger.

These behaviors are common to most, but not all, whales. In the same way, some whales migrate and others do not. Most baleen whales, such as gray, right, and humpback whales, migrate between a winter breeding ground and a summer feeding site.

Migrating whales feed in polar seas, where krill and other zooplankton are plentiful. In the Arctic, this feeding takes place between April and November. Gray whales head south to the coast of Mexico, but hump-back whales winter off the Hawaiian Islands. These whales live in the Northern Hemisphere, the half of the earth above the equator. Whales that live in the Southern

This right whale is lobtailing—raising its tail above the water and slapping it down.

Did You Know?
Fin whales live up to one hundred years. Blue whales live eighty to ninety years. Bowheads may live up to 180 years, although this is not known for certain.

Would You Believe?
Male humpback whales
sing remarkably beautiful
songs to attract their mates.
The songs may last thirty
minutes or more and can
be repeated several times.

Hemisphere move on an opposite sched-
ule. The Southern Hemisphere is the half
of the earth below the equator. There they

*This narwhal has a distinctive, long
tusk, which is actually a tooth.*

feed from December through February, which is summer in the Southern Hemisphere. Thus, whale populations in the two hemispheres head to tropical waters at different times and never meet.

Migrating whales mate and give birth in tropical waters. Whales do not mate for life, and cows often mate with several different bulls while they are in **estrus,** or a fertile period. The length of pregnancy differs from species to species, but most whales carry young for about a year.

As whales grow, they become adults able to produce young. Males reach maturity between four and thirty-five years old. For females, the age of maturity can be between four to twenty-eight years old. For many whales, maturity depends less on age and more on size. Minke whales weigh about 4 or 5 metric tons (4.4 to 5.5 tons) at maturity. Male gray whales are mature at 11 meters (36 feet) long, but Bryde's whales (pronounced BROO-des) become mature at 12.2 meters (40 feet).

Whales become senior citizens when they are about forty years old. However, many whales live long past their fortieth birthdays. Blue whales generally live thirty to ninety years, while fin whales live ninety to one hundred years. Even small beaked whales, such as Baird's beaked whales, can live up to seventy years.

Chapter Four

Whales, Whales, and More Whales

Whales are warm-blooded mammals that have lived in all of the earth's oceans for more than forty million years. They belong to a group of mammals known as **cetaceans** and are close relatives of dolphins and porpoises. In fact, it is often hard to tell a small whale from a dolphin.

Identifying whales can be surprisingly difficult. Yes, it is possible to identify a blue whale because of its size, a beluga because of its white color, or a sperm whale because of its square-shaped head. However, minke, southern bottlenose, and pygmy right whales are roughly the same size. They swim in the same seas, and they have similar-shaped **dorsal** fins.

Would You Believe?
The smallest whale is the size of the average fourth grader. It is the Hector's beaked whale and it measures 1.4 meters (4.5 feet) and weighs 48 kilograms (105 pounds).

BALEEN WHALES

All baleen whales feed on the smallest of sea creatures, yet they grow to be the planet's largest animals. Baleen whales include right whales, gray whales, and **rorqual** whales. The

A southern right whale and her calf feed near the surface.

Did You Know?
The largest whale is the blue whale, measuring on average 25 meters (82 feet) and weighing 90 to 120 metric tons (99 to 132 tons). Blue whales are also the largest creatures ever to live— even bigger than dinosaurs. A blue whale's tongue is the size of an elephant.

term *rorqual* means "groove throat" in Old Norse. This family includes blue, Bryde's, fin, sei, minke, and humpback

A minke whale swims in the waters near Queensland, Australia.

whales. All six species have throat pleats that expand during feeding, much like a pelican's pouch.

The common feature of baleen whales is a comb that works like a strainer. The differences lie in the technique baleen whales use for feeding. Fin, bowhead, right, and sei whales skim their food from the water's surface. Gray whales feed off the ocean bottom. Water flows through the mouth continuously as the whale feeds.

Blue and humpback whales gulp down their food along with gallons of water. They force the water from their mouths and retain the food. Humpbacks force sardines or other small fish into a ball by blowing a screen of bubbles around the outside of a school. The prey gathers close together, making an easy meal for the humpbacks.

TOOTHED WHALES

The differences between baleen and toothed whales are visible in their heads and mouths. Whale teeth are generally cone shaped and vary in size and number, depending on the species. Sperm whales, the largest toothed whales, have the largest teeth. Sperm whales have an upper row of teeth that never erupt from the gums and a lower row of fifty to sixty teeth in a 5-meter (16.4-foot) long jaw. Each tooth weighs about 900 grams (2 pounds).

Narwhals, belugas, and beaked whales also belong to the toothed whale family. Narwhals and belugas are, perhaps, the most distinctive toothed whales. Male narwhals have long tusks. Belugas have white skin that blends in with their snowy Arctic environment.

A Cuvier's beaked whale, one of the many species of toothed whales, surfaces off the coast of North Carolina.

There are twenty-one species of beaked whales, most of which are small to medium in size. Beaked whales live in the open ocean, far from continental shelves, which are relatively shallow areas that extend about 160 to 320 kilometers (100 to 200 miles) off the shores. Beaked whales are called deepwater species. They have small dorsal fins, extended lower jaws, and tail flukes with no central notches. Very little is known about beaked whales. They are hard to find in the wild and even harder to study. Several species live in Antarctic waters in remote areas, where few scientists go.

DOLPHINS AND PORPOISES

A sleek body rides the waves beside the bow of a cruise ship in the Caribbean Sea. In the South Pacific Ocean, a gray figure bursts from the crest of a wave, spins, and drops back into the water. Along Antarctica's coast, a pod of black-and-white animals hunts together, waiting for young sea lions and penguins to enter the surf. These creatures are pantropical spotted dolphins, spinner dolphins, and orcas, which are just a few of the oceanic dolphins.

More than thirty-four species of oceanic dolphins have been identified. Dolphins range in size from orcas (9.5 meters

Did You Know?
In most dolphin species, the males are longer and heavier than the females.

or 31 feet) to small black dolphins (1.6 meters or 5 feet). Some are world travelers, while others prefer to stay close to home. Common dolphins and striped dolphins are found in **temperate** and tropical oceans worldwide. White-beaked dolphins swim the waters of northeastern Canada, Greenland, and Iceland. Some dolphins hunt by forcing small schooling fish into bait balls. Others herd their prey into shore. One thing about oceanic dolphins—they do not live alone. Dolphins are always found in pods.

Four species of river dolphins inhabit freshwater rivers and **estuaries** in South America and Asia. These dolphins live in the Amazon and Plata rivers in South America, the Ganges in India, and the Yangtze in China. River dolphins are seriously affected by water pollution and are the most endangered cetaceans worldwide. The baiji, the Yangtze River dolphin, is believed to be already extinct.

Porpoises and dolphins look alike, but they are not the same animals. Both species belong to the toothed whale family. Porpoises are much smaller than dolphins, seldom measuring longer than 3 meters (9.8 feet). Where dolphins look sleek and slender, porpoises are plump. Porpoises have triangular dorsal fins that look like shark fins and no beaks. Their teeth are shaped like small shovels,

while dolphins have cone-shaped teeth. In terms of their behavior, porpoises are shy, while dolphins are outright nosy. If you are in a boat and a gray cetacean stops by to visit, it is most likely a dolphin.

An eastern spinner dolphin jumps out of the water near Mexico's coast.

Chapter Five

The Past, Present, and Future

What was the first contact between humans and whales? Perhaps an early human stood on the shore and saw a sea creature blowing "smoke" into the air. Possibly a huge creature rose from the water and landed with a crash. These must have been fearsome sights. No wonder humans included whales in myths and legends. By the Middle Ages, pictures of whales began to appear on ocean maps over labels that read "Here there be monsters."

It is most likely that humans first began using whales when whales became stranded on beaches. Humans discovered blubber that could be melted into oil and meat that could be roasted over a fire. The waterproof skin, sinew, bones, and baleen were all put to use. Once humans had boats, hunting whales became a means for humans to survive long, cold winters. That type of hunting had little effect on whale populations.

COMMERCIAL WHALING

Hunting whales for money began as early as the 1100s, when Basque hunters sailed out of Spain's Bay of Biscay. By the 1600s, whaling had become a very profitable business. Whale oil was burned in lamps. Ambergris was sold to perfume makers, and whalebone was used in making ladies' underwear. Builders developed ships that allowed hunters to turn blubber into oil as soon as the whales were killed.

This painting from the 1800s shows a whaling ship hunting a group of whales.

Did You Know?
Right whales got their name because they were the "right" whales to hunt. They moved slowly, provided a large amount of oil, and floated when they died.

Whalers began killing more whales each year than were born. Whaling operations were conducted by the people of Russia, Japan, the countries of South America, and the new colonies in North America. There seemed to be plenty of whales in the oceans, enough to last for centuries.

As ships improved, the distance ships could travel to kill whales increased. Blue whales, sperm whales, right whales, and gray whales from around the globe were harpooned and turned into lamp oil and ointments for wounds.

Clever inventors discovered ways to use whale oil in soap, margarine, and

Would You Believe?
Sperm whales were not hunted for meat or blubber, but for ambergris and spermaceti. Ambergris forms in the whale's belly, coating undigested squid beaks. It is used in making perfume. Spermaceti is an oily compound found in sperm whales' heads that was used in making cosmetics, ointments, and candles.

This style of engraving is called scrimshaw. It was made on the tooth of a sperm whale.

cooking fat. Whale oil became an ingredient in crayons and candles, paints and perfumes, drugs, inks, and waxes. Strips of baleen became parts of hairbrushes, umbrellas, and ladies' bras. A single whale tooth could be turned into a hundred buttons. Even leftover whale parts were useful, too. They were ground up and spread as garden fertilizer.

Most people think whaling ended when people began using electric lights, gas heat, and more comfortable ladies' underwear. Unfortunately for whales, faster ships, mechanical harpoons, and sonar just took whaling to a new level. In the twentieth century, killing and processing whales became so easy, that whaling drove many whale species to the point of extinction.

THE END OF WHALES?

Today, whales suffer from several threats, all connected to humans. Pollution pours into the oceans. Chemical poisons travel on ocean currents. They are found in the flesh of zooplankton and schooling fish—whale food. As whales eat these poisoned creatures, they eat poison. The poison is stored in the blubber, which is turned into milk by whale mothers. Therefore, infants calves nurse on poisoned milk. Eventually, the poison either kills the whales or destroys their ability to produce healthy young.

Despite **conservation** efforts to the contrary, whaling continues. The International Whaling Commission represents a group of nations that once hunted whales. The commission has banned most whaling, particularly the hunting of endangered whale species.

Unfortunately, there are loopholes in the agreement signed by whaling nations. Nations can hunt whales for research, and Japan takes full advantage of that opportunity. In one year, Japan killed fifty whales supposedly for research. The whale meat ended up in Japanese seafood markets. This was not research-driven hunting, but hunting to make money.

Norway and Russia also want to resume commercial whaling. On Russia's Pacific Coast, native Russians can catch whales for **subsistence** purposes. Subsistence hunting

Endangered Whale Species

SPECIES	POPULATION*	STATUS AND LISTINGS**
northern right whale	500–1,000	endangered (ESA, IUCN)
southern right whale	3,000	endangered (ESA); vulnerable (IUCN)
bowhead whale	8,000	endangered (ESA, IUCN)
blue whale	10,000–14,000	endangered (ESA, IUCN)
fin whale	120,000–150,000	endangered (ESA); vulnerable (IUCN)
sei whale	50,000	endangered (ESA)
humpback whale	10,000+	endangered (ESA, IUCN)
sperm whale	200,000	endangered (ESA)
w. n. pacific gray whale	100	endangered (ESA)

*estimates
**ESA=Endangered Specie Act, IUCN=World Conservation Union Red Data book
Source: *www.seaworld.org/animal-info/animal-bytes/animalia/eumetazoa/coelomates/deuterostomes/chordata/craniata/mammalia/cetacea/endangered-whales-fs.htm#table*

means one whale is caught, and the meat and blubber are distributed among villagers. What actually happens is that several whales are killed, and the meat and blubber distributed for profit to Russian cities.

Saving whales seems easy enough. Stop the killing, and they will survive. Humans must also stop polluting the seas. In the same way that nations have created preserves for tigers and elephants, preserves for whales are also needed. Put away the harpoons and shoot whales with cameras. If we continue to destroy nature's balance in our oceans, we will eventually pay the price for our actions.

Scientists put a transmitter on a beluga whale to learn more about its movements and habits.

Glossary

amphipods (AM-fih-podz) small crustaceans

baleen (buh-LEEN) a horny material found in the upper jaws of certain whales

cetaceans (seh-TAY-shuns) marine mammals, including whales, porpoises, and dolphins, with nearly hairless bodies, flippers, and flat, notched tails

conservation (kon-sur-VAY-shun) the preservation or management of natural resources

crustaceans (kruh-STAY-shuns) sea creatures with external skeletons and jointed limbs, such as crabs and shrimps

dorsal (DOR-sul) on the back or upper surface of an organism

echolocation (ek-oh-loh-KAY-shun) the method used by toothed whales and bats to find prey by sending out sounds and tracking the echo

estrus (ESS-truss) a period when a female animal is ready for mating

estuaries (ES-choo-ayr-eez) wide lower courses of rivers that are affected by tides and are a mix of salt water and freshwater

extinct (eks-TINKT) the state of a plant or animal no longer existing

flukes (FLOOKS) either of two horizontal lobes of the tail of a whale

krill (KRIL) tiny, shrimp-like crustaceans that are the primary food of baleen whales

migrating (MY-grayt-ing) moving from one location to another to live

rorqual (ROHR-kwul) any of several members of a family of baleen whales

sediment (SED-uh-munt) material that collects at the bottom of a body of water

silt (SILT) tiny bits of soil and rock that can be found floating in water and in sediment

subsistence (sub-SIS-tenss) hunting or growing crops purely for one's own use, without any surplus

temperate (TEM-per-ut) having weather that is not extremely hot or extremely cold

zooplankton (zoh-uh-PIANGK-tun) very small animals that float in water

For More Information

Watch It

Awesome Whales for Kids, DVD (Mechanicsburg, PA: The Whale Video Company, 2006)

Humpback Whales, VHS (Arlington, VA: PBS Home Video, 2000)

In the Wild: Gray Whales, VHS (Arlington, VA: PBS Home Video, 1995)

Whales: An Unforgettable Journey, DVD (Burbank, CA: Slingshot Entertainment, 2000)

Read It

Becker, John. *Gray Whales*. Farmington Hills, MI: KidHaven Press, 2004.

Carwardine, Mark. *Whales & Dolphins*. New York: DK Adult, 2002.

Ihimaera, Witi. *The Whale Rider*. New York: Harcourt Children's Books, 2003.

Johnson, Christina. *Blue Whales and Other Baleen Whales*. Chicago: World Book, 2005.

Kerrod, Robin. *Whales and Dolphins*. London: Southwater Publishing, 2001.

MacMillan, Dianne M. *Humpback Whales*. Minneapolis, MN: Lerner Publications, 2003.

Spilsbury, Louise and Richard. *Blue Whale*. Chicago: Heinemann Library, 2006.

Look It Up

Visit our Web page for lots of links about whales:
http://www.childsworld.com/links

Note to Parents, Teachers, and Librarians: We routinely verify our Web links to make sure they are safe, active sites—so encourage your readers to check them out!

The Animal Kingdom
Where Do Whales Fit In?

Kingdom: Animalia

Phylum: Chordata (animals with backbones)

Class: Mammalia

Order: Cetacea

Suborders:

Mysticeti (baleen whales)

Odontoceti (toothed whales)

Families:

Balaenidae (right whales)

Balaenopteridae (rorquals)

Eschrichtiidae (gray whales)

Monodontidae (narwhals)

Neobalaenidae (pygmy right whales)

Physeteridae (sperm whales)

Ziphiidae (beaked whales)

Index

About the Author

Sophie Lockwood is a former teacher and a longtime writer. She writes textbooks, newspaper articles, and magazine articles. Sophie enjoys writing about animals and their habits. The most interesting part of her research, Sophie says, is learning how scientists apply their knowledge to save endangered species. She lives with her husband in the foothills of the Blue Ridge Mountains.